MANAGEMENT MAVEN

THE ART OF EFFECTIVE LEADERSHIP AND
TEAM EMPOWERMENT

NANCY BARLOW

Copyright © 2024 by Nancy Barlow

All rights reserved. No part of this book may be reproduced, stored in a retrieval system, or transmitted, in any form or by any means, electronic, mechanical, photocopying, recording, or otherwise, without the prior written permission of the author, except in the case of brief quotations embodied in critical reviews and certain other noncommercial uses permitted by copyright law.

TABLE OF CONTENT

INTRODUCTION 5

CHAPTER 1: UNDERSTANDING EFFECTIVE LEADERSHIP 7

    1.1   The Evolution of Leadership Theories 9

    1.2   Characteristics of Successful Leaders 13

    1.3   Leadership Styles and Their Impact 18

CHAPTER 2: BUILDING TRUST AND COMMUNICATION 23

    2.1 The Importance of Trust in Leadership 24

    2.2 Effective Communication Strategies 29

    2.3 Creating a Culture of Openness and Transparency 34

CHAPTER 3: EMPOWERING YOUR TEAM FOR SUCCESS 40

    3.1 Delegating Responsibilities Effectively 41

    3.2 Encouraging Autonomy and Accountability 46

3.3 Recognizing and Developing Talent Within the Team 51

CHAPTER 4: NAVIGATING CHALLENGES AND CONFLICT RESOLUTION 57

4.1 Understanding Common Team Challenges 59

4.2 Strategies for Conflict Resolution 63

4.3 Turning Challenges into Opportunities for Growth 68

CHAPTER 5: FOSTERING INNOVATION AND GROWTH 73

5.1 Cultivating a Culture of Innovation 75

5.2 Leveraging Diversity for Creative Solutions 80

5.3 Sustaining Long-Term Growth and Adaptability 85

CONCLUSION 91

INTRODUCTION

"Management Maven: The Art of Effective Leadership and Team Empowerment" delves into the core principles that define exceptional leadership in today's dynamic business landscape. In a world where leadership is not just about authority but also about inspiration and collaboration, this book serves as a guide for aspiring and seasoned leaders alike. Through insightful strategies, real-world examples, and practical advice, readers will explore the intricacies of fostering a culture of empowerment, trust, and innovation within their teams.

This book goes beyond traditional leadership paradigms, focusing on holistic approaches that nurture both individual growth and team cohesion. From mastering effective communication and conflict resolution to leveraging diversity and fostering a growth mindset, "Management Maven" equips leaders with the tools they need to navigate complex challenges and drive meaningful change.

Whether you're a manager looking to enhance your leadership skills or an entrepreneur building a high-performing team, this book offers actionable insights and proven techniques to help you become a true maven of management. Join the ranks of successful leaders who understand that true leadership is not just about directing; it's about empowering others to achieve greatness.

CHAPTER 1: UNDERSTANDING EFFECTIVE LEADERSHIP

In Chapter 1 of "Management Maven: The Art of Effective Leadership and Team Empowerment," we embark on a journey to unravel the intricacies of leadership in today's dynamic world. Effective leadership is not merely a position of authority but a nuanced blend of skills, traits, and strategies that inspire and guide teams toward success.

We begin by delving into the evolution of leadership theories, tracing how our understanding of leadership has evolved over time. From traditional hierarchical models to contemporary approaches emphasizing collaboration and empowerment, we explore the diverse paths that have shaped modern leadership paradigms.

Next, we examine the essential characteristics of successful leaders. Through insightful analysis and real-world examples, we uncover the key traits that set exceptional leaders apart, from emotional intelligence and adaptability to vision and resilience.

Furthermore, we delve into various leadership styles and their impact on teams and organizational outcomes. By understanding the strengths and limitations of different leadership approaches, readers gain valuable insights into choosing and adapting their leadership style to suit diverse situations and challenges.

Join us as we navigate the fascinating landscape of effective leadership, equipping you with the knowledge and tools to lead with confidence, empathy, and strategic vision.

1.1 The Evolution of Leadership Theories

The evolution of leadership theories spans centuries and reflects the changing dynamics of societies, organizations, and human understanding. This evolution is characterized by shifts in emphasis from traits to behaviors, situational factors, and contextual influences. Let's comprehensively discuss the major phases in the evolution of leadership theories:

1. **Trait Theory Era (Early 20th Century):**

   - **Focus:** This era focused on identifying innate traits that distinguish effective leaders from others. Traits like intelligence, charisma, decisiveness, and integrity were believed to be inherent to successful leadership.

   - **Key Figures:** Early scholars such as Thomas Carlyle and Ralph Stogdill laid the foundation for trait theory, which later evolved with contributions from researchers like Kurt Lewin, who emphasized leadership qualities and skills.

2. **Behavioral Theories (Mid-20th Century):**

   - **Shift:** Behavioral theories shifted the focus from innate traits to observable behaviors. Researchers argued that effective leadership could be learned and developed through specific behaviors rather than being purely innate.

   - **Contributions:** The work of Kurt Lewin, Douglas McGregor, and Blake and Mouton's Managerial Grid contributed significantly to this shift. Concepts like the Ohio State Studies and the University of Michigan Studies differentiated between task-oriented and relationship-oriented behaviors in leaders.

3. **Contingency and Situational Theories (Late 20th Century):**

   - **Contextual Considerations:** Contingency and situational theories introduced the idea that effective leadership is contingent upon various situational factors. Leadership effectiveness depends on the context, followers' characteristics, and the nature of tasks.

- **Key Models:** Hersey and Blanchard's Situational Leadership Model, Fiedler's Contingency Theory, and House's Path-Goal Theory are prominent examples. These models emphasize adapting leadership styles based on situational demands and follower readiness.

4. **Transformational and Transactional Leadership (Late 20th Century - Present):**

- **Focus on Vision and Inspiration:** Transformational leadership theory emphasizes leaders' ability to inspire and motivate followers towards a shared vision. It highlights qualities like charisma, vision, and emotional intelligence.

- **Transactional Aspects:** Transactional leadership, on the other hand, focuses on exchanges between leaders and followers, emphasizing rewards, punishments, and clear expectations.

- **Modern Perspectives:** Contemporary theories often blend aspects of transformational, transactional, and servant leadership, recognizing the complexity of leadership in today's global and diverse environments.

5. **Emerging Trends:**

- **Authentic and Servant Leadership:** Recent years have seen a growing interest in authentic leadership, emphasizing transparency, ethical decision-making, and self-awareness. Servant leadership also emphasizes leaders' focus on serving the needs of others and fostering a culture of empathy and collaboration.

- **Adaptive Leadership:** With the rapid pace of change and complexity in modern organizations, adaptive leadership theories have gained traction. These theories focus on leaders' ability to navigate uncertainty, facilitate change, and foster innovation in dynamic environments.

Overall, the evolution of leadership theories reflects a continuous quest to understand what makes leaders effective in diverse contexts. From early trait-based approaches to modern, context-sensitive theories, the study of leadership continues to evolve, incorporating insights from psychology, sociology, organizational behavior, and management studies.

1.2 Characteristics of Successful Leaders

Successful leaders possess a diverse array of characteristics that enable them to inspire, guide, and achieve exceptional results. These characteristics are not solely innate but can be developed and refined through experience, self-awareness, and continuous learning. Let's comprehensively discuss the key characteristics of successful leaders:

1. **Visionary and Strategic Thinking:**

   - Successful leaders have a clear vision of the future and a strategic mindset to set goals and navigate complexities.

- They can anticipate trends, identify opportunities, and formulate effective strategies to achieve long-term objectives.

2. **Effective Communication:**

- Strong communication skills are essential for successful leaders to articulate their vision, motivate teams, and foster collaboration.

- They listen actively, convey ideas clearly, and adapt their communication style to resonate with diverse audiences.

3. **Empathy and Emotional Intelligence:**

- Successful leaders understand and empathize with the emotions and perspectives of others, building trust and fostering a positive organizational culture.

- They possess emotional intelligence, which includes self-awareness, self-regulation, social awareness, and relationship management.

4. **Decisiveness and Accountability:**

- Effective leaders make timely and informed decisions, taking calculated risks when necessary.

- They take responsibility for their actions and outcomes, holding themselves and others accountable for performance and results.

5. **Adaptability and Resilience:**

- Successful leaders adapt to changing circumstances, embrace innovation, and learn from failures and setbacks.

- They demonstrate resilience, maintaining composure and motivating others during challenges and adversity.

6. **Empowerment and Collaboration:**

- Leaders empower and delegate responsibilities, trusting their teams to take ownership and contribute meaningfully.

- They foster a collaborative environment, valuing diverse perspectives, and promoting teamwork and collective achievement.

7. **Integrity and Ethics**:

- Ethical leadership is paramount for success, as leaders uphold integrity, honesty, and ethical conduct in all interactions and decisions.

- They prioritize ethical considerations, earning trust and respect from stakeholders.

8. **Continuous Learning and Development:**

- Successful leaders are lifelong learners, continuously seeking knowledge, feedback, and opportunities for personal and professional growth.

- They invest in their development and that of their teams, cultivating a culture of learning and innovation.

9. **Responsible and Sustainable Leadership:**

   - In today's global context, successful leaders prioritize sustainability, responsible business practices, and social impact.

   - They consider the broader implications of their actions, contributing to sustainable growth and societal well-being.

10. **Inspiration and Motivation:**

    - Successful leaders inspire and motivate others, fostering enthusiasm, commitment, and a shared sense of purpose.

    - They lead by example, embodying the values and behaviors they expect from their teams.

By embodying these characteristics, successful leaders not only drive organizational success but also create environments where individuals can thrive, innovate, and contribute meaningfully to collective goals.

1.3 Leadership Styles and Their Impact

Leadership styles play a crucial role in shaping organizational culture, driving performance, and influencing the overall effectiveness of teams. Different leadership styles have distinct characteristics and impact on employee motivation, satisfaction, and productivity. Let's comprehensively discuss various leadership styles and their impact:

1. **Autocratic Leadership:**

   - **Characteristics:** Autocratic leaders make decisions independently, with little input from team members. They maintain strict control over tasks and processes.

   - **Impact:** While this style can be effective in situations requiring quick decisions and clear direction, it may lead to low morale, reduced creativity, and limited employee engagement due to lack of autonomy.

2. Democratic Leadership:

- **Characteristics:** Democratic leaders involve team members in decision-making, value input and feedback, and encourage participation in goal-setting.

- **Impact:** This style fosters a sense of ownership, empowerment, and collaboration among team members. It promotes innovation, boosts morale, and enhances job satisfaction.

3. Laissez-Faire Leadership:

- **Characteristics:** Laissez-faire leaders adopt a hands-off approach, providing minimal guidance or supervision. They trust employees to manage their own tasks and decisions.

- **Impact:** While this style can promote autonomy and creativity in self-motivated teams, it may lead to confusion, lack of direction, and inefficiency in less disciplined or inexperienced teams.

4. **Transactional Leadership:**

   - **Characteristics:** Transactional leaders focus on exchanges with team members, using rewards and punishments to motivate performance. They emphasize clear roles, rules, and performance expectations.

   - **Impact:** This style can be effective in achieving short-term goals and maintaining performance standards. However, it may hinder innovation and intrinsic motivation, as it relies heavily on external incentives.

5. **Transformational Leadership:**

   - **Characteristics:** Transformational leaders inspire and motivate followers through a compelling vision, charisma, and emotional intelligence. They empower and develop their teams, fostering trust and commitment.

   - **Impact:** This style leads to higher levels of employee engagement, creativity, and loyalty. It promotes a shared vision, encourages continuous improvement, and drives long-term organizational success.

6. Servant Leadership:

- **Characteristics:** Servant leaders prioritize the needs of their team members, serving as mentors, coaches, and facilitators. They focus on empathy, listening, and supporting individual growth.

- **Impact:** This style fosters a culture of trust, collaboration, and employee well-being. It encourages ethical behavior, teamwork, and a strong sense of community, leading to higher job satisfaction and retention.

7. Charismatic Leadership:

- **Characteristics:** Charismatic leaders inspire and influence others through their personality, vision, and persuasive communication skills. They energize and mobilize teams toward shared goals.

- **Impact:** While charismatic leadership can be motivational and effective in rallying teams, it may also rely heavily on the leader's personality, potentially leading to dependency and challenges in sustaining momentum without the leader's presence.

8. **Adaptive Leadership:**

   - **Characteristics:** Adaptive leaders thrive in complex and changing environments, demonstrating flexibility, resilience, and problem-solving skills. They adapt strategies and behaviors to meet evolving challenges.

   - **Impact:** This style promotes agility, innovation, and organizational resilience. Adaptive leaders empower teams to navigate uncertainty, embrace change, and seize opportunities for growth and adaptation.

Each leadership style has its strengths and limitations, and effective leaders often blend aspects of different styles based on situational demands, organizational culture, and the needs of their teams. A versatile leader understands when to be directive, participative, supportive, or visionary, leveraging diverse styles to maximize impact and achieve sustainable success.

CHAPTER 2: BUILDING TRUST AND COMMUNICATION

Chapter 2 of "Management Maven: The Art of Effective Leadership and Team Empowerment" delves into the fundamental pillars of successful leadership: building trust and fostering effective communication. In today's interconnected and rapidly changing business landscape, trust and communication are the cornerstones that underpin strong relationships, collaboration, and organizational success.

Effective leaders understand that trust is not a given but must be earned through consistency, transparency, and integrity. Trust creates a foundation of reliability and mutual respect, enabling teams to work cohesively towards common goals. Similarly, communication serves as the lifeblood of organizational dynamics, facilitating clarity, alignment, and engagement among team members.

In this chapter, we explore the strategies, techniques, and best practices for cultivating trust and enhancing communication within teams. From fostering open dialogue and active listening to promoting transparency and empathy, we delve into the essential elements that contribute to a culture of trust and effective communication.

Join us as we navigate the intricate nuances of building trust and communication in leadership, equipping you with practical insights and actionable strategies to strengthen relationships, drive engagement, and empower your team for success.

2.1 The Importance of Trust in Leadership

The importance of trust in leadership cannot be overstated, as it forms the foundation for healthy relationships, effective collaboration, and organizational success. Trust is a dynamic element that permeates all levels of an organization, influencing employee engagement, productivity, and retention. Let's comprehensively discuss the significance of trust in leadership:

1. **Enhanced Communication and Transparency:**

- Trust fosters open communication and transparency within teams and across organizational hierarchies. When employees trust their leaders, they feel comfortable sharing ideas, concerns, and feedback, leading to better decision-making and problem-solving.

2. **Increased Employee Engagement and Morale:**

- Trusting relationships between leaders and team members contribute to higher levels of employee engagement and morale. When employees trust their leaders, they are more likely to feel valued, motivated, and committed to organizational goals.

3. **Effective Conflict Resolution:**

- Trust enables constructive conflict resolution, as team members feel safe expressing differing viewpoints and resolving conflicts collaboratively. Leaders who prioritize trust create environments where conflicts are viewed as opportunities for growth and innovation rather than sources of tension.

4. **Empowerment and Autonomy:**

- Trusted leaders empower their teams by delegating responsibilities and granting autonomy. When employees trust their leaders' judgment and intentions, they feel empowered to make decisions, take initiative, and contribute meaningfully to organizational success.

5. **Building Strong Teams and Relationships:**

- Trust is essential for building strong teams and fostering positive relationships among team members. Trusting environments promote cooperation, camaraderie, and a sense of belonging, leading to higher levels of teamwork and collaboration.

6. **Retention and Loyalty:**

   - Trustworthy leadership contributes to higher employee retention and loyalty. When employees trust their leaders, they are more likely to stay with the organization, contribute their best efforts, and advocate for the company as brand ambassadors.

7. **Risk-Taking and Innovation:**

   - Trust encourages risk-taking and innovation, as employees feel supported in exploring new ideas and experimenting with creative solutions. Trusted leaders create a culture where calculated risks are embraced, failures are viewed as learning opportunities, and innovation thrives.

8. **Resilience in Times of Change:**

   - During periods of change, trust in leadership is crucial for navigating uncertainty and maintaining organizational resilience. Trusted leaders inspire confidence, provide clear direction, and guide teams through transitions with integrity and empathy.

9. Ethical Leadership and Organizational Integrity:

- Trustworthy leaders uphold ethical standards and promote organizational integrity. When leaders act with honesty, fairness, and ethical conduct, they earn the trust and respect of their teams, stakeholders, and the broader community.

In essence, trust is the cornerstone of effective leadership, creating a positive work environment where individuals thrive, teams excel, and organizations achieve sustainable success. Leaders who prioritize trust invest in building strong relationships, fostering open communication, and demonstrating consistency, integrity, and empathy in their actions.

2.2 Effective Communication Strategies

Effective communication is essential for successful leadership, team collaboration, and organizational effectiveness. It involves conveying information clearly, listening actively, and fostering open dialogue to ensure understanding and alignment among team members. Let's comprehensively discuss various effective communication strategies:

1. Clear and Concise Messaging:

- Communicate messages in a clear, concise, and straightforward manner to avoid ambiguity and misunderstanding. Use simple language, avoid jargon, and prioritize clarity to ensure that information is easily comprehensible to all team members.

2. **Active Listening:**

   - Actively listen to understand others' perspectives, concerns, and ideas. Practice empathy, maintain eye contact, ask clarifying questions, and provide feedback to demonstrate that you value and respect others' input.

3. **Open and Transparent Communication:**

   - Foster a culture of open and transparent communication where team members feel comfortable sharing information, feedback, and concerns. Encourage honesty, address issues promptly, and promote a sense of trust and accountability.

4. **Two-Way Communication:**

   - Promote two-way communication by encouraging dialogue and soliciting input from team members. Create opportunities for feedback, brainstorming sessions, and collaborative discussions to foster engagement and participation.

5. **Adapt Communication Style:**

   - Adapt your communication style to suit the preferences and needs of different team members. Consider factors such as cultural background, personality traits, and communication preferences to ensure effective communication across diverse audiences.

6. **Use of Visual Aids:**

   - Utilize visual aids such as charts, graphs, diagrams, and presentations to enhance understanding and convey complex information more effectively. Visual elements can complement verbal communication and facilitate retention of key concepts.

7. **Feedback and Recognition:**

   - Provide constructive feedback, recognition, and praise to reinforce positive behaviors and performance. Acknowledge contributions, celebrate achievements, and address areas for improvement to promote continuous learning and growth.

8. **Clarify Expectations and Goals:**

   - Clearly communicate expectations, goals, roles, and responsibilities to ensure alignment and accountability within the team. Set SMART (Specific, Measurable, Achievable, Relevant, Time-bound) goals and regularly communicate progress and updates.

9. **Use of Technology:**

   - Leverage technology tools such as email, messaging platforms, video conferencing, and project management software to facilitate communication, collaboration, and information sharing, especially in virtual or remote work environments.

10. **Empathetic Communication:**

    - Practice empathetic communication by considering others' feelings, perspectives, and experiences. Show empathy, understanding, and support in your interactions to build trust, rapport, and positive relationships.

11. **Conflict Resolution Skills:**

- Develop effective conflict resolution skills to address disagreements and tensions constructively. Use active listening, empathy, mediation, and negotiation techniques to facilitate resolution and promote a positive work environment.

12. **Continuous Improvement:**

- Continuously evaluate and refine your communication strategies based on feedback, outcomes, and evolving needs. Solicit input from team members, seek opportunities for learning and development, and adapt your approach to optimize communication effectiveness.

By implementing these effective communication strategies, leaders can foster a culture of clarity, collaboration, and trust, leading to enhanced team performance, innovation, and organizational success.

2.3 Creating a Culture of Openness and Transparency

Creating a culture of openness and transparency is crucial for fostering trust, collaboration, and organizational success. Such a culture encourages honest communication, promotes accountability, and empowers employees to contribute their best ideas and efforts. Let's comprehensively discuss the strategies and benefits of creating a culture of openness and transparency:

1. **Clear Communication Policies:**

   - Establish clear communication policies and guidelines that promote openness and transparency within the organization. Communicate expectations regarding sharing information, addressing concerns, and maintaining confidentiality.

2. **Lead by Example:**

- Leaders play a critical role in creating a culture of openness and transparency. Lead by example by communicating openly, soliciting feedback, and being receptive to diverse perspectives. Demonstrate honesty, integrity, and ethical behavior in all interactions.

3. **Encourage Dialogue and Feedback:**

- Encourage open dialogue and feedback across all levels of the organization. Create channels for employees to voice their opinions, share ideas, and raise concerns without fear of reprisal. Actively listen to feedback and take appropriate action to address issues.

4. **Promote Information Sharing:**

- Promote information sharing by providing access to relevant data, resources, and updates. Foster a culture where knowledge and information are shared openly, enabling informed decision-making and collaboration.

5. **Transparency in Decision-Making:**

   - Be transparent about decision-making processes, rationale, and outcomes. Communicate the reasons behind decisions, involve stakeholders when appropriate, and seek input to ensure decisions are well-informed and understood.

6. **Open-Door Policy:**

   - Implement an open-door policy where employees feel comfortable approaching leaders with questions, suggestions, or concerns. Create a supportive environment where feedback is valued, and ideas are welcomed.

7. **Training and Development:**

   - Provide training and development programs that emphasize the importance of openness, transparency, and effective communication. Equip employees with the skills and tools they need to communicate clearly, collaborate effectively, and navigate conflicts constructively.

8. **Celebrate Successes and Learn from Failures:**

- Celebrate successes and achievements openly to recognize contributions and reinforce positive behaviors. Similarly, encourage learning from failures and mistakes by fostering a culture where lessons learned are shared openly and used to improve processes and outcomes.

9. **Accountability and Trust:**

- Foster accountability by setting clear expectations, holding individuals accountable for their actions, and addressing issues transparently. Build trust by demonstrating consistency, reliability, and integrity in your words and actions.

10. **Embrace Diversity and Inclusion:**

- Embrace diversity and inclusion in communication practices by respecting diverse perspectives, promoting equity, and creating a culture where everyone feels valued and heard. Encourage cross-functional collaboration and teamwork to leverage diverse strengths and experiences.

11. **Continuous Improvement:**

   - Continuously evaluate and improve communication practices to enhance openness and transparency. Solicit feedback from employees, measure communication effectiveness, and implement changes based on insights and lessons learned.

Benefits of Creating a Culture of Openness and Transparency:

- Enhanced trust and credibility among employees, customers, and stakeholders.

- Increased employee engagement, morale, and job satisfaction.

- Improved decision-making, problem-solving, and innovation.

- Stronger relationships, collaboration, and teamwork.

- Greater organizational agility, adaptability, and resilience in times of change.

By prioritizing openness and transparency in communication practices, organizations can cultivate a positive work culture that fosters trust, empowers employees, and drives sustainable success.

CHAPTER 3: EMPOWERING YOUR TEAM FOR SUCCESS

Chapter 3 of "Management Maven: The Art of Effective Leadership and Team Empowerment" delves into the transformative power of empowering your team for success. Empowerment is not just about delegating tasks; it's about fostering a culture of trust, autonomy, and accountability that unleashes the full potential of each team member.

In this chapter, we explore the strategies, principles, and best practices for empowering your team to achieve greatness. From delegating responsibilities effectively to encouraging autonomy and recognizing talent within the team, we delve into the essential elements that contribute to a high-performing and empowered team.

Empowering your team goes beyond traditional leadership approaches; it requires empathy, active listening, and a genuine commitment to supporting individual growth and development. By empowering your team members, you not only enhance their job satisfaction and engagement but also drive innovation, collaboration, and organizational success.

Join us as we navigate the empowering journey, equipping you with practical insights and actionable strategies to cultivate a culture of empowerment, trust, and excellence within your team.

3.1 Delegating Responsibilities Effectively

Delegating responsibilities effectively is a fundamental aspect of leadership that enables leaders to leverage their team's strengths, foster autonomy, and achieve collective goals efficiently. Effective delegation involves assigning tasks, empowering team members, providing support and guidance, and holding individuals accountable for outcomes. Let's comprehensively discuss the strategies and benefits of delegating responsibilities effectively:

1. **Clear Communication and Expectations:**

   - Clearly communicate tasks, responsibilities, deadlines, and expectations when delegating. Provide detailed instructions, clarify objectives, and ensure that team members understand the scope and importance of their assignments.

2. **Match Tasks with Skills and Abilities:**

   - Assign tasks based on each team member's skills, strengths, and capabilities. Match responsibilities with individuals who have the necessary expertise, experience, and interest to ensure successful execution.

3. **Empowerment and Trust:**

   - Empower team members by granting them autonomy and decision-making authority within their delegated tasks. Trust their judgment, encourage creative problem-solving, and provide support and resources as needed.

4. **Provide Adequate Resources and Support:**

- Ensure that team members have access to the resources, information, and training necessary to complete their delegated tasks effectively. Offer guidance, coaching, and feedback to support their progress and development.

5. **Set Clear Goals and Milestones:**

- Define clear goals, milestones, and success criteria for delegated tasks. Break down complex projects into manageable stages, monitor progress regularly, and provide feedback to keep individuals on track.

6. **Encourage Accountability and Ownership:**

- Foster a culture of accountability by holding team members accountable for their delegated responsibilities. Encourage ownership of tasks, promote a sense of pride in accomplishments, and recognize and celebrate achievements.

7. Delegate Authority, Not Just Tasks:

- Delegate authority along with tasks, allowing team members to make decisions and take initiative within their delegated roles. Empowering individuals with decision-making power fosters innovation, creativity, and a sense of ownership.

8. Monitor and Provide Feedback:

- Monitor the progress of delegated tasks, provide ongoing feedback, and offer support or guidance as needed. Address any challenges or issues promptly to ensure successful outcomes and continuous improvement.

9. Encourage Collaboration and Communication:

- Foster collaboration and communication among team members by encouraging sharing of ideas, insights, and best practices. Create opportunities for collaboration, brainstorming sessions, and knowledge sharing to enhance collective effectiveness.

10. **Evaluate and Learn from Delegation:**

- After tasks are completed, evaluate the outcomes, gather feedback from team members, and identify lessons learned. Use insights from delegation experiences to improve future delegation processes and refine leadership approaches.

Benefits of Delegating Responsibilities Effectively:

- Increased productivity and efficiency by leveraging team strengths and capabilities.

- Enhanced job satisfaction and engagement among team members through empowerment and autonomy.

- Improved decision-making and problem-solving by tapping into diverse perspectives and skills.

- Development of leadership skills and delegation capabilities among leaders and team members.

- Strengthened teamwork, collaboration, and accountability within the organization.

By mastering the art of effective delegation, leaders can unlock the full potential of their teams, foster a culture of empowerment and accountability, and achieve collective success efficiently.

3.2 Encouraging Autonomy and Accountability

Encouraging autonomy and accountability among team members is key to fostering a high-performing and empowered team. Autonomy allows individuals to make decisions, take ownership of their work, and contribute creatively, while accountability ensures that they are responsible for their actions, outcomes, and commitments. Let's comprehensively discuss strategies for encouraging autonomy and accountability:

1. **Define Clear Goals and Expectations:**

   - Clearly define goals, objectives, and expectations for each team member. Provide a roadmap outlining priorities, deadlines, and key deliverables to guide autonomous decision-making and accountability.

2. **Empower Decision-Making:**

   - Empower team members to make decisions within their areas of responsibility. Encourage them to explore solutions, take initiative, and innovate while aligning their decisions with organizational goals and values.

3. **Provide Guidance and Support:**

   - Offer guidance, resources, and support to help team members succeed autonomously. Provide training, mentorship, and access to information and tools that enable informed decision-making and effective problem-solving.

4. **Encourage Risk-Taking and Learning:**

   - Create a culture that encourages calculated risk-taking and continuous learning. Embrace failures as learning opportunities, encourage experimentation, and recognize efforts to drive innovation and growth.

5. **Clarify Roles and Responsibilities:**

   - Clarify roles, responsibilities, and decision-making authority to avoid ambiguity and promote accountability. Ensure that each team member understands their contribution to overall objectives and the impact of their work on team success.

6. **Set SMART Goals:**

   - Establish SMART (Specific, Measurable, Achievable, Relevant, Time-bound) goals that empower individuals to take ownership and track progress independently. Encourage self-assessment and reflection to gauge performance against established criteria.

7. **Promote Collaboration and Communication:**

   - Foster collaboration and communication among team members to support autonomy and accountability. Encourage sharing of ideas, best practices, and feedback to promote a culture of continuous improvement and mutual support.

8. **Recognize and Reward Results:**

- Recognize and reward individual and team achievements based on results, contributions, and adherence to accountability. Acknowledge efforts that demonstrate initiative, innovation, and commitment to driving positive outcomes.

9. **Hold Regular Feedback Sessions:**

- Conduct regular feedback sessions to discuss progress, challenges, and opportunities for improvement. Provide constructive feedback, celebrate successes, and address areas for development to reinforce accountability and promote growth.

10. **Lead by Example:**

- Lead by example by demonstrating autonomy, accountability, and responsible decision-making in your own work. Model ethical behavior, transparency, and resilience, and showcase the benefits of autonomy and accountability to inspire others.

Benefits of Encouraging Autonomy and Accountability:

- Increased employee engagement, motivation, and job satisfaction.

- Improved decision-making, problem-solving, and innovation.

- Enhanced productivity and efficiency through empowered and responsible teams.

- Strengthened trust, collaboration, and communication within the organization.

- Development of leadership skills, self-reliance, and ownership among team members.

By fostering autonomy and accountability, leaders create an environment where individuals thrive, contribute meaningfully, and drive collective success with a sense of ownership and commitment.

3.3 Recognizing and Developing Talent Within the Team

Recognizing and developing talent within the team is crucial for maximizing individual potential, fostering a culture of growth and learning, and driving organizational success. Effective talent recognition and development strategies involve identifying strengths, providing opportunities for growth, offering mentorship and support, and creating a conducive environment for continuous learning and skill enhancement. Let's comprehensively discuss these aspects:

1. **Identifying Talent:**

   - Start by identifying talent within the team through performance evaluations, feedback from peers and supervisors, and assessments of skills, competencies, and potential. Look for individuals who demonstrate exceptional abilities, initiative, and a strong work ethic.

2. Providing Opportunities for Growth:

  - Offer opportunities for talent development and growth, such as challenging assignments, projects, leadership roles, training programs, and professional development initiatives. Create a career path that aligns with individuals' interests, aspirations, and strengths.

3. Offering Mentorship and Coaching:

  - Pair talented individuals with experienced mentors or coaches who can provide guidance, feedback, and support. Mentorship programs facilitate knowledge transfer, skill development, and career guidance, enhancing individuals' professional growth and success.

4. Creating a Conducive Environment:

  - Foster a supportive and inclusive environment that values diversity, collaboration, and continuous learning. Encourage teamwork, creativity, and innovation, and provide resources and tools that facilitate talent development and knowledge sharing.

5. Recognizing Achievements and Contributions:

- Recognize and celebrate the achievements and contributions of talented individuals within the team. Acknowledge their efforts, talents, and successes publicly to boost morale, motivation, and job satisfaction.

6. Encouraging Continuous Learning:

- Promote a culture of continuous learning and skill development by offering access to training programs, workshops, certifications, and educational resources. Encourage individuals to pursue learning opportunities that align with their career goals and areas of interest.

7. Empowering Individuals with Responsibility:

- Empower talented individuals with responsibilities that challenge and stretch their capabilities. Delegate meaningful tasks, projects, or leadership roles that allow them to showcase their talents, take initiative, and contribute strategically to organizational objectives.

8. Providing Feedback and Growth Opportunities:

- Offer regular feedback, performance reviews, and growth opportunities to talented individuals. Identify areas for improvement, provide constructive feedback, and collaborate on development plans that address skill gaps and enhance performance.

9. Encouraging Collaboration and Networking:

- Encourage collaboration, networking, and knowledge sharing among talented individuals and across teams. Facilitate cross-functional projects, peer learning sessions, and networking events to foster collaboration and expand professional networks.

10. Promoting Leadership Development:

- Invest in leadership development programs for talented individuals who show leadership potential. Provide opportunities to lead teams, mentor others, and participate in leadership training to prepare them for future leadership roles within the organization.

Benefits of Recognizing and Developing Talent Within the Team:

- Enhanced employee engagement, motivation, and retention.

- Improved team performance, productivity, and innovation.

- Strengthened leadership pipeline and succession planning.

- Increased organizational agility, adaptability, and competitiveness.

- Cultivation of a positive and growth-oriented organizational culture.

By recognizing and developing talent within the team, organizations can unlock the full potential of their workforce, drive individual and collective success, and build a resilient and high-performing team that contributes to long-term organizational excellence.

CHAPTER 4: NAVIGATING CHALLENGES AND CONFLICT RESOLUTION

Chapter 4 of "Management Maven: The Art of Effective Leadership and Team Empowerment" delves into the intricate dynamics of navigating challenges and mastering conflict resolution within teams. In any organizational setting, challenges and conflicts are inevitable, but how leaders navigate and resolve them can significantly impact team performance, morale, and overall success.

In this chapter, we explore the strategies, principles, and best practices for effectively navigating challenges and resolving conflicts in a constructive and positive manner. From understanding the root causes of conflicts to implementing conflict resolution techniques and fostering a culture of collaboration and mutual respect, we delve into the essential elements that contribute to a harmonious and productive team environment.

Navigating challenges requires resilience, adaptability, and effective problem-solving skills, while conflict resolution demands empathy, active listening, and a commitment to finding win-win solutions. By equipping leaders and team members with the tools and strategies to address challenges and conflicts proactively, organizations can strengthen relationships, promote trust, and enhance team cohesion.

Join us as we navigate the complex terrain of challenges and conflicts, providing practical insights, real-world examples, and actionable techniques to help you navigate obstacles with confidence, foster positive relationships, and steer your team towards collective success.

4.1 Understanding Common Team Challenges

Understanding common team challenges is essential for leaders and organizations to effectively address issues, foster collaboration, and ensure team success. These challenges can range from communication issues to conflicts, lack of motivation, and productivity barriers. Let's comprehensively discuss some of the most common team challenges and strategies to mitigate them:

1. **Communication Barriers:**

   - Communication breakdowns can hinder collaboration and productivity. Address this challenge by promoting open communication channels, encouraging active listening, providing clear instructions, and using multiple communication tools to ensure messages are understood.

2. **Conflict and Disagreements:**

   - Conflicts and disagreements can arise due to different perspectives, goals, or personalities within the team. Foster a culture of respect, empathy, and open dialogue to address conflicts constructively. Encourage team members to express concerns, find common ground, and work towards mutually beneficial solutions.

3. **Lack of Clarity and Direction:**

   - Unclear goals, roles, and expectations can lead to confusion and disengagement. Provide clear direction, set SMART goals, define roles and responsibilities, and communicate expectations transparently to ensure everyone understands their contributions to team objectives.

4. **Poor Team Dynamics:**

   - Team dynamics can suffer from cliques, favoritism, or lack of trust. Encourage collaboration, diversity of thought, and inclusivity within the team. Foster a supportive environment where every team member feels valued, respected, and included in decision-making processes.

5. Low Morale and Motivation:

- Low morale and motivation can result from factors such as lack of recognition, burnout, or unclear career growth paths. Boost morale by recognizing and celebrating achievements, providing opportunities for skill development and career advancement, and promoting work-life balance.

6. Task Delegation and Time Management:

- Challenges with task delegation and time management can lead to inefficiencies and missed deadlines. Delegate tasks effectively based on team members' strengths and workload capacities. Set realistic timelines, prioritize tasks, and use time management techniques to optimize productivity.

7. Resistance to Change:

- Resistance to change can hinder innovation and adaptation to new processes or technologies.

Address resistance by involving team members in decision-making, communicating the benefits of change, providing training and support, and acknowledging concerns and feedback.

8. Lack of Accountability:

- Accountability issues can arise when team members do not take ownership of their responsibilities or outcomes. Establish clear accountability measures, set performance expectations, provide feedback on progress, and recognize and reward accountability and results.

9. Cultural and Diversity Challenges:

- Cultural differences, diversity challenges, and language barriers can impact communication and collaboration. Promote cultural awareness, inclusivity, and diversity training to foster understanding, respect, and effective teamwork across diverse backgrounds.

10. **Resource Constraints:**

   - Limited resources, budget constraints, or technological limitations can impede progress and innovation. Prioritize resource allocation, seek opportunities for cost-effective solutions, and collaborate with stakeholders to leverage available resources optimally.

By understanding and addressing these common team challenges proactively, leaders can build resilient, high-performing teams that overcome obstacles, leverage strengths, and achieve collective success. Regular assessments, feedback mechanisms, and continuous improvement initiatives can also contribute to addressing evolving challenges and enhancing team effectiveness over time.

4.2 Strategies for Conflict Resolution

Conflict resolution is a critical skill for leaders and team members to navigate differences, promote understanding, and foster collaboration within teams. Effective conflict resolution strategies help resolve disputes constructively, improve communication, and strengthen relationships. Let's comprehensively discuss some key strategies for conflict resolution:

1. **Open Communication:**

   - Encourage open and honest communication to address conflicts proactively. Create a safe space for team members to express their concerns, perspectives, and emotions without fear of judgment or reprisal. Actively listen to understand others' viewpoints and demonstrate empathy.

2. **Identify Root Causes:**

   - Identify the underlying causes of conflict, such as miscommunication, differing expectations, personality clashes, or resource constraints. Clarify misunderstandings, gather facts, and explore the reasons behind conflicting opinions or behaviors to find common ground.

3. **Focus on Interests, Not Positions:**

- Shift the focus from positions or demands to underlying interests, needs, and goals. Encourage collaborative problem-solving by seeking win-win solutions that address everyone's interests and concerns. Explore creative options and alternatives to resolve conflicts mutually.

4. **Use Constructive Feedback:**

- Provide constructive feedback to address behaviors or actions contributing to conflict. Use "I" statements to express feelings and observations objectively, avoid blaming or accusing language, and focus on specific behaviors that need improvement. Offer feedback in private and with a focus on finding solutions.

5. **Practice Active Listening:**

- Practice active listening by paying attention to verbal and nonverbal cues, summarizing key points, and asking clarifying questions to ensure understanding. Validate others' perspectives and emotions, demonstrate empathy, and show genuine interest in finding resolution.

6. **Seek Mediation or Facilitation:**

   - Consider involving a neutral mediator or facilitator to help parties resolve conflicts impartially. A mediator can facilitate discussions, manage emotions, and guide the process towards mutually acceptable solutions. Ensure that the mediator remains neutral, fair, and focused on collaboration.

7. **Collaborative Problem-Solving:**

   - Encourage collaborative problem-solving by involving all parties in brainstorming solutions, evaluating options, and reaching consensus. Encourage creativity, flexibility, and compromise to find solutions that meet everyone's needs and priorities.

8. **Set Clear Expectations and Agreements:**

   - Clarify expectations, roles, and responsibilities to prevent future conflicts. Establish clear agreements or ground rules for communication, decision-making, and conflict resolution processes within the team. Ensure that everyone understands their roles in maintaining a positive team environment.

9. **Manage Emotions Effectively:**

   - Help team members manage emotions effectively during conflicts. Encourage self-awareness, emotional regulation, and constructive expression of feelings. Provide tools and techniques for managing stress, frustration, and conflict-related emotions.

10. **Follow-Up and Evaluation:**

    - Follow up on conflict resolution efforts to ensure that agreements are upheld and conflicts do not resurface. Monitor progress, solicit feedback from team members, and evaluate the effectiveness of conflict resolution strategies. Adjust approaches as needed to address ongoing or new conflicts.

By implementing these conflict resolution strategies, leaders and team members can effectively address conflicts, build trust, improve communication, and create a positive and collaborative team environment. Conflict, when managed well, can lead to growth, innovation, and strengthened relationships within teams.

4.3 Turning Challenges into Opportunities for Growth

Turning challenges into opportunities for growth is a transformative approach that empowers individuals and organizations to learn, innovate, and thrive in the face of adversity. Instead of viewing challenges as setbacks, this mindset reframes them as valuable learning experiences and catalysts for personal and professional development. Let's comprehensively discuss strategies for turning challenges into opportunities for growth:

1. **Embrace a Growth Mindset:**

   - Cultivate a growth mindset that sees challenges as opportunities for learning and improvement. Encourage individuals to embrace challenges, persist in the face of setbacks, and view failures as stepping stones to success.

2. **Identify Learning Objectives:**

   - Identify specific learning objectives or lessons to be gained from challenges. Encourage reflection, self-assessment, and goal-setting to extract meaningful insights and skills development from challenging experiences.

3. **Seek Feedback and Support:**

   - Seek feedback from peers, mentors, or experts to gain different perspectives and insights on how to overcome challenges. Leverage support networks, coaching, or mentorship to develop skills, enhance capabilities, and navigate obstacles effectively.

4. **Adaptability and Resilience:**

   - Foster adaptability and resilience in individuals and teams to cope with change and uncertainty. Encourage flexible thinking, adaptability to new circumstances, and the ability to bounce back from setbacks stronger than before.

5. **Encourage Innovation and Creativity:**

   - Encourage innovative thinking and creative problem-solving to find novel solutions to challenges. Create a culture that values experimentation, risk-taking, and embracing new ideas to drive innovation and growth.

6. **Collaborative Approach:**

   - Foster collaboration and teamwork to leverage diverse perspectives, skills, and strengths in overcoming challenges. Encourage cross-functional collaboration, knowledge sharing, and collective problem-solving to generate innovative solutions.

7. **Set Realistic Goals and Milestones:**

- Set realistic goals and milestones to track progress and measure success in addressing challenges. Break down larger challenges into manageable tasks, prioritize action steps, and celebrate small wins along the way to maintain motivation and momentum.

8. **Continuous Learning and Development:**

- Promote continuous learning and development by providing access to training, resources, and opportunities for skill enhancement. Encourage individuals to pursue professional development, acquire new knowledge, and expand their capabilities to tackle challenges effectively.

9. **Adopt a Solutions-Oriented Mindset:**

- Adopt a solutions-oriented mindset that focuses on finding actionable solutions rather than dwelling on problems. Encourage proactive problem-solving, critical thinking, and decision-making to address challenges efficiently and effectively.

10. Celebrate Success and Growth:

- Celebrate successes and growth achievements resulting from overcoming challenges. Recognize and reward individuals and teams for their efforts, resilience, and innovative solutions. Use success stories as inspiration and motivation for future challenges.

11. Evaluate and Iterate:

- Evaluate the outcomes and lessons learned from turning challenges into opportunities for growth. Identify areas for improvement, gather feedback, and iterate strategies and approaches to enhance effectiveness in addressing future challenges.

By adopting these strategies, individuals and organizations can transform challenges into opportunities for personal and professional growth, innovation, and resilience. Embracing a positive mindset, fostering collaboration, and promoting continuous learning are key pillars in leveraging challenges as catalysts for positive change and development.

CHAPTER 5: FOSTERING INNOVATION AND GROWTH

Chapter 5 of "Management Maven: The Art of Effective Leadership and Team Empowerment" delves into the dynamic realm of fostering innovation and driving growth within teams and organizations. In today's rapidly evolving business landscape, innovation is not just a buzzword but a strategic imperative for staying competitive, adapting to change, and creating value for customers and stakeholders.

In this chapter, we explore the strategies, principles, and best practices for fostering a culture of innovation and driving sustainable growth. From cultivating creativity and embracing experimentation to fostering collaboration and leveraging technology, we delve into the essential elements that fuel innovation and propel organizations forward.

Fostering innovation is not solely the responsibility of R&D departments or top leadership; it requires active participation and empowerment at all levels of the organization. By nurturing a culture that values curiosity, diversity of thought, and continuous learning, leaders can unleash the full potential of their teams and unlock innovative solutions to complex challenges.

Join us as we embark on a journey of exploration and discovery, uncovering the secrets to fostering innovation, driving growth, and creating a future-ready organization. Whether you're a seasoned leader or an aspiring innovator, this chapter offers insights, strategies, and actionable steps to inspire creativity, spark innovation, and catalyze growth within your team and organization.

5.1 Cultivating a Culture of Innovation

Cultivating a culture of innovation is essential for organizations to thrive in today's dynamic and competitive business environment. A culture that fosters innovation encourages creativity, collaboration, experimentation, and continuous learning, leading to breakthrough ideas, improved processes, and sustainable growth. Let's comprehensively discuss strategies for cultivating a culture of innovation:

1. **Leadership Commitment:**

   - Leadership plays a pivotal role in fostering an innovative culture. Leaders should demonstrate a strong commitment to innovation, set a clear vision and goals, allocate resources, and create an environment that values and rewards creativity and risk-taking.

2. **Encourage Curiosity and Exploration:**

   - Encourage curiosity and a thirst for learning among employees. Create opportunities for exploration, experimentation, and brainstorming. Embrace diverse perspectives, encourage asking questions, and challenge the status quo to spark innovative thinking.

3. **Promote Psychological Safety:**

   - Foster a psychologically safe environment where employees feel comfortable expressing ideas, sharing feedback, and taking calculated risks. Encourage open communication, active listening, and constructive feedback to nurture trust and collaboration.

4. **Empowerment and Autonomy:**

   - Empower employees with the autonomy to make decisions, take ownership of projects, and pursue innovative ideas. Provide resources, support, and a clear framework for experimentation and innovation while allowing room for creativity and initiative.

5. **Cross-Functional Collaboration:**

   - Foster cross-functional collaboration and interdisciplinary teamwork to leverage diverse perspectives, skills, and experiences. Create platforms, such as innovation labs, hackathons, or cross-departmental projects, that encourage collaboration and knowledge sharing.

6. **Continuous Learning and Skill Development:**

   - Promote a culture of continuous learning and skill development to equip employees with the knowledge, tools, and techniques needed for innovation. Provide access to training, workshops, and learning resources that focus on creativity, design thinking, and problem-solving.

7. **Embrace Failure as Learning:**

   - Encourage a mindset that views failure as a learning opportunity and stepping stone to success. Normalize experimentation, iterate quickly, learn from failures, and celebrate lessons learned. Create a culture where employees feel safe to take risks and learn from setbacks.

8. **Customer-Centric Approach:**

   - Foster a customer-centric approach to innovation by understanding customer needs, gathering feedback, and co-creating solutions with customers. Encourage empathy, user research, and design-led thinking to drive innovation that delivers value and meets customer expectations.

9. **Recognize and Reward Innovation:**

   - Recognize and reward innovative ideas, contributions, and outcomes. Celebrate successes, showcase innovative projects, and acknowledge individuals or teams that drive meaningful change and impact through their innovative efforts.

10. **Iterative Improvement:**

    - Embrace an iterative approach to innovation by continuously refining and improving processes, products, and services based on feedback and insights. Encourage experimentation, gather data-driven feedback, and iterate rapidly to drive continuous improvement and innovation.

11. **Promote Diversity and Inclusion:**

- Foster a diverse and inclusive environment that values different perspectives, backgrounds, and experiences. Diversity sparks creativity and innovation by bringing together varied viewpoints and ideas. Encourage inclusivity, equity, and belonging to unleash the full potential of your diverse workforce.

12. **Measure and Evaluate Innovation:**

- Establish metrics, KPIs, and feedback mechanisms to measure innovation efforts and outcomes. Track key indicators such as idea generation, implementation success, impact on business goals, and employee engagement with innovation initiatives. Use data to inform decision-making and drive continuous innovation.

By implementing these strategies, organizations can create a culture that embraces innovation as a core value, empowers employees to think creatively, and fosters an environment where breakthrough ideas thrive. Cultivating a culture of innovation is an ongoing journey that requires commitment, continuous effort, and a shared vision of driving positive change and growth.

5.2 Leveraging Diversity for Creative Solutions

Leveraging diversity for creative solutions is a powerful strategy that harnesses the unique perspectives, experiences, and talents of a diverse workforce to drive innovation, problem-solving, and business success. Diversity encompasses differences in race, ethnicity, gender, age, culture, background, skills, and more, and when effectively leveraged, it can lead to creative thinking, improved decision-making, and enhanced competitiveness. Let's comprehensively discuss how organizations can leverage diversity for creative solutions:

1. **Diverse Perspectives and Insights:**

   - Diversity brings together a range of perspectives, viewpoints, and insights that can lead to innovative solutions. Embrace diversity as a source of creativity, encouraging employees to share their unique experiences, ideas, and approaches to problem-solving.

2. **Cognitive Diversity:**

   - Foster cognitive diversity by bringing together individuals with different thinking styles, problem-solving approaches, and cognitive strengths. Encourage analytical thinkers, creative thinkers, strategic thinkers, and empathetic thinkers to collaborate and complement each other's strengths.

3. **Inclusive Decision-Making:**

   - Promote inclusive decision-making processes that value and integrate diverse viewpoints. Encourage open dialogue, active listening, and collaborative decision-making to leverage the collective intelligence of diverse teams and avoid groupthink.

4. **Cross-Functional Collaboration:**

   - Foster cross-functional collaboration across diverse teams and departments to leverage complementary skills, knowledge, and expertise. Create opportunities for interdisciplinary teamwork, knowledge sharing, and collective problem-solving to generate creative solutions.

5. **Design Thinking and User-Centric Approach:**

   - Embrace design thinking methodologies and a user-centric approach to innovation that prioritizes understanding diverse customer needs, preferences, and experiences. Incorporate user research, empathy mapping, and co-creation with diverse stakeholders to design solutions that meet diverse user needs effectively.

6. **Diversity of Skills and Talents:**

   - Recognize and leverage the diverse skills, talents, and strengths of your workforce. Encourage cross-training, skill-sharing, and mentorship programs that allow employees to learn from each other, collaborate on projects, and apply their unique expertise to solve complex challenges.

7. **Cultural Intelligence:**

   - Develop cultural intelligence (CQ) among employees to navigate cultural differences effectively and leverage cultural diversity for creative solutions. Provide cultural awareness training, promote cross-cultural communication, and foster a culture of respect, empathy, and inclusivity.

8. **Diversity in Leadership and Decision-Making Roles:**

   - Promote diversity in leadership and decision-making roles to ensure that diverse perspectives are represented at all levels of the organization. Encourage diverse leadership teams, inclusive decision-making processes, and mentorship programs that support diverse talent development and advancement.

9. **Innovation Labs and Hackathons:**

   - Create innovation labs, hackathons, or idea incubators that bring together diverse teams to brainstorm, ideate, and prototype innovative solutions. Provide resources, support, and recognition for innovative ideas that emerge from these collaborative initiatives.

10. Data-Driven Insights:

- Use data-driven insights to understand the impact of diversity on innovation and creative solutions. Analyze diversity metrics, employee feedback, and innovation outcomes to identify patterns, trends, and opportunities for leveraging diversity effectively.

11. Continuous Learning and Improvement:

- Foster a culture of continuous learning and improvement that values feedback, reflection, and adaptation. Encourage employees to learn from successes and failures, iterate on ideas, and embrace a growth mindset that embraces diversity as a driver of innovation and creativity.

By leveraging diversity for creative solutions, organizations can tap into the full potential of their diverse workforce, drive innovation, enhance problem-solving capabilities, and create a competitive advantage in today's diverse and dynamic business landscape. Embrace diversity as a strategic asset that fuels creativity, fosters collaboration, and drives positive change within your organization.

5.3 Sustaining Long-Term Growth and Adaptability

Sustaining long-term growth and adaptability is crucial for organizations to remain competitive, resilient, and relevant in an ever-evolving business landscape. Long-term growth involves achieving sustainable financial performance, expanding market reach, and continuously creating value for customers and stakeholders. Adaptability, on the other hand, is the ability to respond effectively to changing market conditions, technological advancements, and customer preferences. Let's comprehensively discuss strategies for sustaining long-term growth and adaptability:

1. **Strategic Planning and Vision:**

   - Develop a clear strategic plan and vision that outlines long-term goals, priorities, and strategies for growth. Align organizational objectives with market trends, customer needs, and emerging opportunities to sustain growth and drive innovation.

2. **Market Research and Customer Insights:**

   - Conduct ongoing market research and gather customer insights to understand market dynamics, competitive landscape, and customer preferences. Use data-driven analysis to identify growth opportunities, anticipate market trends, and make informed strategic decisions.

3. **Innovation and Product Development:**

   - Foster a culture of innovation and continuous improvement to drive product development, service enhancements, and new offerings. Invest in research and development, collaborate with cross-functional teams, and leverage technology to innovate and stay ahead of competitors.

4. Agile and Adaptive Strategies:

- Adopt agile and adaptive strategies that allow for flexibility, rapid decision-making, and course corrections in response to changing market conditions. Embrace experimentation, iterate on ideas, and pivot quickly to capitalize on emerging opportunities or address challenges.

5. Talent Development and Leadership:

- Invest in talent development, leadership capabilities, and succession planning to build a skilled and adaptable workforce. Develop leaders who can inspire, motivate, and lead teams through change, foster innovation, and drive sustainable growth strategies.

6. Customer-Centric Approach:

- Prioritize a customer-centric approach that focuses on delivering value, exceeding customer expectations, and building long-term relationships. Listen to customer feedback, gather insights, and tailor products, services, and experiences to meet evolving customer needs and preferences.

7. **Partnerships and Collaboration:**

   - Foster strategic partnerships, alliances, and collaborations with industry peers, startups, suppliers, and stakeholders to expand market reach, access new markets, and leverage complementary strengths. Collaborate on innovation projects, joint ventures, and co-creation initiatives to drive growth and innovation.

8. **Digital Transformation and Technology Adoption:**

   - Embrace digital transformation initiatives and leverage technology advancements to optimize processes, enhance customer experiences, and drive operational efficiency. Embrace automation, data analytics, artificial intelligence, and cloud technologies to innovate and stay competitive.

9. **Risk Management and Resilience:**

   - Implement robust risk management practices, contingency plans, and resilience strategies to mitigate potential threats, disruptions, and uncertainties. Build organizational resilience by diversifying revenue streams, maintaining financial stability, and adapting to changing market dynamics.

10. Measuring Performance and Continuous Improvement:

- Establish key performance indicators (KPIs), metrics, and benchmarks to measure performance, track progress, and evaluate the effectiveness of growth strategies. Use data analytics and performance insights to identify areas for improvement, optimize processes, and drive continuous innovation.

11. Corporate Social Responsibility (CSR) and Sustainability:

- Integrate corporate social responsibility (CSR) initiatives and sustainability practices into business operations to enhance brand reputation, attract socially conscious customers, and contribute positively to society and the environment. Align CSR efforts with long-term growth objectives and stakeholder expectations.

12. Adaptive Culture and Change Management:

- Foster an adaptive culture that embraces change, encourages learning, and empowers employees to adapt to new challenges and opportunities. Implement effective change management practices, communicate transparently, and involve employees in decision-making to facilitate organizational agility and resilience.

By implementing these strategies and fostering a culture of innovation, adaptability, and continuous improvement, organizations can sustain long-term growth, navigate challenges effectively, and seize opportunities for success in a rapidly changing business environment. Embrace change as a catalyst for growth, leverage diverse strengths, and stay agile to thrive in the long term.

CONCLUSION

In conclusion, "Management Maven: The Art of Effective Leadership and Team Empowerment" is a testament to the power of visionary leadership, collaborative teamwork, and continuous innovation in driving organizational success. Throughout this book, we have explored the fundamental principles, strategies, and best practices that empower leaders to inspire greatness in themselves and their teams.

Effective leadership is not just about managing tasks; it's about inspiring vision, fostering trust, and empowering individuals to reach their full potential. By cultivating a culture of innovation, embracing diversity, and prioritizing adaptability, leaders can navigate challenges, capitalize on opportunities, and sustain long-term growth in a dynamic business landscape.

As we conclude this journey, I encourage you to apply the insights, strategies, and lessons learned from this book in your leadership journey. Lead with integrity, empathy, and resilience. Empower your team members, foster collaboration, and embrace change as a catalyst for growth and innovation.

Remember, great leadership is an ongoing journey of learning, growth, and evolution. Stay curious, embrace challenges, and inspire excellence in yourself and others. Together, we can create a future where effective leadership and empowered teams drive meaningful impact and success.

Thank you for embarking on this transformative journey with "Management Maven." May your leadership journey be filled with purpose, impact, and continuous growth.

www.ingramcontent.com/pod-product-compliance
Lightning Source LLC
Chambersburg PA
CBHW070201230526
45471CB00002B/771